FOOD & FEASTS

IN
ANCIENT
EGYPT

Richard Balkwill

new Discovery
B·O·O·K·S
New York

First American publication 1994 by New Discovery Books, Macmillan Publishing Company, 866 Third Avenue, New York, NY 10022

Macmillan Publishing Company is part of the Maxwell Communication Group of Companies.

First published in 1994 in Great Britain by Wayland (Publishers) Ltd

A ZOË BOOK

Devised and produced by
Zoë Books Limited
15 Worthy Lane
Winchester
Hampshire SO23 7AB
England

Printed in Belgium by Proost N.V.
Design: Jan Sterling, Sterling Associates
Picture research: Victoria Sturgess
Map: Gecko Limited
Production: Grahame Griffiths

10 9 8 7 6 5 4 3 2 1

Silver Burdett 11.22 1/97

Library of Congress Cataloging-in-Publication Data

Balkwill, Richard.
   Food & feasts in ancient Egypt / Richard Balkwill.
     p. cm. —(Food & feasts)
   Includes index.
   ISBN 0-02-726323-1
   1. Diet—Egypt—Juvenile literature. 2. Cookery, Egyptian—Juvenile literature. 3. Food habits—Egypt—Juvenile literature. 4. Egypt—Social life and customs—To 332 B.C.—Juvenile literature. [1. Cookery, Egyptian. 2. Food habits—Egypt. 3. Egypt—Social life and customs—To 332 B.C.]. I. Title. II. Title: Food and feasts in ancient Egypt. III. Series.
TX360.E3B35 1994
394.1'0932—dc20   94-4706

Summary: A social history of what kinds of foods the Ancient Egyptians ate, how they ate it, and how their lives were conditioned by the Nile River.

Photographic acknowledgments

The publishers wish to acknowledge, with thanks, the following photographic sources:

Ancient Art & Architecture Collection 5l&r, 8t, 10t, 11t, 13t&c, 21b, 22t; Bolton Museum & Art Gallery 17c&b, 19t (model made by Mr H. Ewings of Bury), 20tr, 21c, 23t; Charles Amos Cummings Bequest Fund, courtesy Museum of Fine Arts, Boston 19b; British Museum 9t, 10c, 11c, 18t, 19t, 24t&b; C.M.Dixon title page, 3, 7b, 9b, 11b, 12b, 13b, 14t, 15t, 18b, 20b, 25t&b; Michael Holford 4; Mansell Collection 6b, 8b, 17t, 20tl, 21t; Popperfoto 6t, 7t; Rijksmuseum van Oudheden 16t; Werner Forman Archive 12t, 15b, 16b, 22b; Werner Forman Archive / British Museum 23b / Egyptian Museum, Berlin 14b.

Cover: Ancient Art and Architecture Collection center right; Bolton Museum & Art Gallery top left; C.M.Dixon center top & left, bottom right.

The publishers have made every effort to trace the copyright holders, but if they have inadvertently overlooked any, they will be pleased to make the necessary arrangement at the first opportunity.

Contents

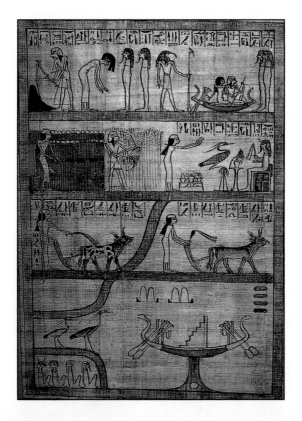

Introduction

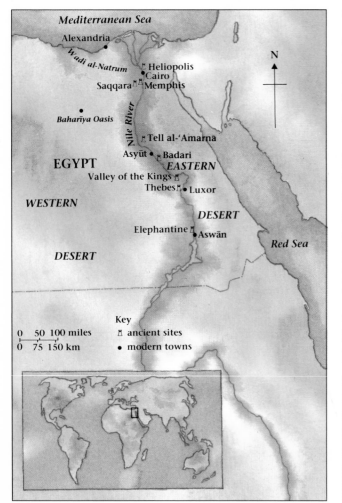

F ive thousand years ago, the country we know today as Egypt was ruled by a king named Menes. Legend says that he was the first king of the human race. The people of his country lived, as many do today, on either side of the Nile River, the longest river in the world.

The history of Ancient Egypt covers the period from about 3000 to 1000 years B.C. B.C. stands for Before (the birth of) Christ, in the Christian calendar. Historians of Egypt, known as Egyptologists, have divided this time into three main sections. They are called the Old Empire, the Middle Empire, and the New Empire. Egypt was ruled by kings and queens. The groups of royal families were called **dynasties**. Each dynasty lasted from two hundred to three hundred years, but we cannot be sure about the exact dates.

Period	Date	Dynasties
Old Empire	3000–2000 B.C.	1–10
Middle Empire	2000–1500 B.C.	11–17
New Empire	1500–1000 B.C.	18–20

△ This map of Egypt shows that most of the land is desert. Many ancient sites and modern towns are in the Nile Valley, the main area for farming.

▷ Huge **pyramids** were built in the Egyptian desert. They were tombs for kings and queens who were buried inside, with food, drink, and treasures as offerings to the gods.

△ King Tutankhamen and his queen, Ankhesenamen. Tutankhamen died in about 1340 B.C. At this time rulers were not buried in pyramids, but in tombs in the Valley of the Kings, near Thebes.

The kings of the Old Empire, who had names like Khufu, Khafre, and Menkaure, built many of the tombs, or pyramids, that are familiar sights in Egypt today. When King Ramses III died at the end of the New Empire, and Egypt became part of Libya and Assyria, more than 2,000 years had passed. That is longer than the time since Britain was part of the Roman Empire, or since Christ was born.

△ In this wall painting from a tomb in Thebes you can see food offerings of animals, birds, and fish.

Pyramids and tombs

The pyramids were built as burial chambers for the rulers of Ancient Egypt. Rulers or noble people in Egypt spent much of the time preparing for death. They thought of death as a journey to the next world and an everlasting afterlife. Their families would provide food for the journey and gifts to the gods.

These **funerary offerings** were placed in the tomb with the body, which was tightly wrapped in cloth. Wall paintings and carvings were made. These pictures tell us a lot about the food people ate. They also show scenes of people fishing and hunting. Rolls of **papyrus**, a reed made into a type of paper, also show pictures and writing. The writing is in the form of symbols known as **hieroglyphs**. The letters form words that are like tiny pictures. The hiero-glyph for the word "smell" is a picture of a nose. The same symbol means "enjoy."

Because the inside of the tomb was dry and airless, many of the gifts, paintings, and papyrus rolls have survived. People who study buildings and objects from the past are called **archaeologists**. Those who **excavate** the tombs today can piece together the way a rich Egyptian lived.

Almost 2,500 years ago, the Greek historian Herodotus wrote about "the gift of the Nile." The Nile River was and is the lifeline of Egypt. As the Nile flows through Egypt, the sun burns down from a clear blue sky. Much of the country on either side is desert. It almost never rains, except in the region near the Mediterranean Sea. Each year, in June, the river level begins to rise. Rain and melting snow flow from the mountains many miles to the south. During September and October in Ancient Egypt, the river rose to a point where it overflowed its banks and flooded large areas of the land. The flood was called the **inundation**.

When the river level fell again, a thick covering of mud or silt was left behind. This made rich, **fertile** ground in which crops could easily be grown. During the flood, water was kept back in lakes, and channels were built to **irrigate**, or carry, water to dry areas a long way from the river. A tool called a shadoof was used to raise water from the river and store it.

△ This shows what the land along the Nile probably looked like during the annual flood.

▽ A shadoof was made by tying a bucket on a rope to one end of a beam, or strong piece of wood. This was held up by a prop and balanced by a heavy weight like a rock or stone. The person using the shadoof would pull on the rope to lift the full bucket from the river or lake.

The Nile River flows for 4,185 miles (6,695 kilometers) from its sources in Central Africa to the Mediterranean Sea. It is made up of two rivers, the Blue Nile, which rises at Lake Tana in Ethiopia, and the White Nile, which rises at Lake Victoria. The White Nile flows north from Uganda and joins the Blue Nile at Khartoum, in Sudan.

A good flood was said to be 16 ells high. An ell was based on the length of a man's arm. It was later a cloth measure of 45 inches, or about 1.1 meters. An old "nilometer" used to stand in the ancient city of Elephantine, with a statue of a boy. The boy has climbed up to the sixteenth ell. He is standing on a rich harvest of corn, vegetables, and fruit.

◁ The large boat is moved along by sails and the oars of many rowers.

The importance of the Nile

The flooding of the river was the most important event each year. The new year in Ancient Egypt was fixed to start on September 15. On that date, the flood was usually at its highest point. Sometimes the flooding was quite small. People called this a "low Nile." The channels that carried the water did not fill up. Crops were not watered, and they died. Food was scarce and people were hungry. When the flooding was very great—a "high Nile"—crops would sometimes be covered in water and were ruined. Carefully dug channels and waterworks might be washed away.

The words for "travel" in Ancient Egypt were *chont*, "go upstream" and *chod*, "go downstream."

The Nile River was important to everyone who lived in Ancient Egypt. Things grew well in the mud and silt left behind by the flood. Fish swam in the river, and animals made their homes in the reeds and swamp beside it. The river was the only quick way of moving any distance.

▽ This drawing, from about 1250 B.C., shows a small boat being paddled along the Nile.

Food and farming

△ Here people are harvesting wheat with **sickles**.

Corn, or grain, was very important to the people of Egypt. Royal workers were paid in corn. Scenes carved in tombs show people buying and selling, or **bartering**, with corn. Even the level of taxes that people had to pay was decided by the amount of corn grown that year.

In November, when the waters of the Nile dropped again, a rich black silt was left behind. The people of Ancient Egypt then began planting seeds of corn. The corn was probably the grain of wheat and barley. Writers tell us that the people used pigs to walk over the ground and press it down. The corn grew and was harvested the following April.

Most years the Egyptians grew more corn than they needed. Other countries knew how fertile Egypt was, and travelers from far away came to buy corn. In the Bible, Jacob tells his sons "I have heard that there is corn in Egypt." (Genesis, chapter 42). In ancient times, Egypt was sometimes called the breadbasket of the world.

▽ This drawing starts from the right. It is taken from a wall painting and shows people gathering the corn grains and separating them out, or winnowing them. A **scribe** is taking note of the amount of corn being taken.

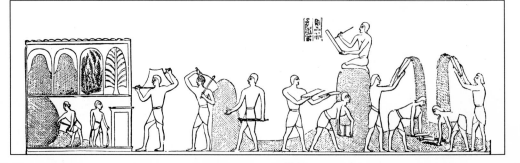

◁ The people in this model, from about 2000 B.C., are grinding corn, sifting flour, kneading dough, and baking bread.

Barley and wheat grains were used as basic food by most people. Whole grains were used to thicken soups. Crushed grain was often mixed with water to make a kind of porridge. It was also stirred with oil and baked on a fire to make a kind of hard cake, like a flapjack. Most of it was ground into flour to make bread.

▽ A wooden model, made around 2400 B.C., of a girl making bread.

Making flour and bread

Many carvings and pictures show how Egyptians made corn into flour. People would grind or pound the corn on a flat stone with another, smoother stone. At first, servants knelt on the ground to do this. Later on, the work was done at a table.

Bread was made by mixing this coarse flour with water. It was then flattened and baked over a fire. The fire was built inside a cone of Nile mud, about three feet (one meter) high. Flames came out of holes in the top of the cone. In the countryside, shepherds looking after their animals baked bread in the ashes of their open fires. Sometimes sand got into the flour, or husks and bits of corn were left in it. Bodies that have been preserved in tombs from this time have teeth that may have been ground

People may have found out by accident that yeast, which is carried in the air, makes bread rise. Risen, or leavened, bread is light because there is more air in it. The uncooked mixture, or **dough**, is malleable and easier to work with, so bakers could make all sorts of shapes with it. They also added milk or eggs to the mixture to make the bread richer, and honey or dates to sweeten it.

▷ Wild ducks nesting in the papyrus are disturbed by a hunter. A cat climbs the reeds to take the eggs.

▽ Bakers made bread in different shapes and sizes. The most common was a triangular bread, called *ta*.

When yeast mixtures were used to make bread, a small piece would be kept from one day to the next to make the dough rise. Pieces of bread were also used in making beer.

down by chewing on rough bread.

What plants grew in Ancient Egypt, besides corn? What animals lived in the marshes near the river? Again, the carvings and paintings of the day tell us a lot about what Egyptians grew, ate, and drank.

For ordinary people in Egypt, bread and vegetables were the main foods, with beer to drink. They did not eat much meat. Most animals were hunted, killed, and eaten by the rulers and the rich people. Egyptians also caught birds and fish in the land surrounding their palaces.

The most common vegetable was probably the bean. Along with peas and lentils, beans of all kinds have been grown in Egypt for thousands of years. Garbanzo beans were ground into flour and added to bread dough. Mashing garbanzo beans and adding sesame seed oil gives us the tasty spread known as hummus. It was as popular in Egypt then as it is today. Lima beans and lentils were also common. People liked young papyrus shoots. Vegetables were sometimes pickled to make them last longer.

Fruits

Dates from palm trees were popular. They were sometimes added to bread or cakes for flavor, and they were also quite easy to keep for long periods. Fresh figs were gathered from thorny fig trees.

Lunch for a worker might have been an onion, or a radish, perhaps some garlic, and a piece of bread. There are signs that cucumbers and even melons were grown—but the color and shape are hard to tell from the pictures!

▷ Date palms and *dom* palms were common trees in Egypt and a good source of fruit.

The Egyptians also grew vines. The grapes were eaten at great feasts, or **banquets**, but were also made into wine. Many fruits that we eat today, such as oranges and lemons, were not grown in Egypt at this time. Sometimes apples and pears were brought in from other countries. Olives were not grown and nuts were rare.

We do not know much about how fruit and vegetables were grown. It seems likely that people grew their food on small plots of land. These were irrigated by channels or by water from tanks filled by shadoofs. Only the rich families in big palaces had gardens.

Monuments from the time show flowers, shady trees, and walled gardens, almost like a park. Vines and fish ponds were common. The lotus flower with its beautiful scent was grown and used at feasts. Wreaths or buds of the flower were placed in guests' hair as they sat at the table.

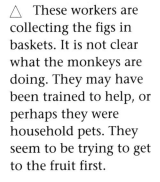

△ These workers are collecting the figs in baskets. It is not clear what the monkeys are doing. They may have been trained to help, or perhaps they were household pets. They seem to be trying to get to the fruit first.

▽ This picture from a Theban tomb shows a fish pond and trees in a rich family's garden. The artist has painted what was in, as well as on, the pond.

Fishing and hunting

▷ There are many hooks on the end of this fishing line. The net has many fish in it, but they look quite small. This may just be so that they will fit into the carving.

Most ordinary people ate fish, ducks, geese, and other wildfowl. There were many fish in the Nile River and in the channels and lakes along the river. People chased the fish into shallow water to spear them or catch them in a net. Lines with many hooks were used, as well as **baited** traps.

The reed beds along the river were full of many different kinds of birds. Ducks and geese were common and can be seen there today, but there were also egrets, storks, and cranes. The person with the job of catching birds for food was the wildfowler. He had to spear them, or make a trap. He could also force them into a corner and throw a large draw net over them. Pictures of wildfowlers show that they

Once caught, fish were cut open and cleaned. To make them last longer, they were often hung up to dry in the hot sun or buried in the sand. Sometimes fish were salted or pickled in oil.

▷ In this carving, a dragnet is being used. Corks keep the net afloat. The fishermen are dragging the net through the water and seem to have made a big catch.

▷ Most houses would have two or three big greyhounds called *slughi*. The dogs were valuable to hunters because they could run faster than a gazelle and were not afraid of lions or leopards.

△ In this picture men are using a mongoose to trap birds.

sometimes worked together.

The nobles of Ancient Egypt hunted for pleasure as well as for food. They chased antelopes, gazelles, and other wild **game**. Sheep and goats were hunted, too. In the desert, away from the river, there were lions and leopards.

The rulers of Egypt thought that the finest game was wild cattle. They hunted the cattle because they thought the meat tasted delicious. These animals could not run fast and must have been quite easy to catch. Often dozens of cattle would be killed at a time, far more than even the people at important feasts could have managed to eat.

Much of the country around the Nile had been covered by marshes and tropical forests. Many of these were turned into fields to grow crops, but some old riverbeds remained. Here thick papyrus reeds grew, hiding wildfowl as well as hippopotamuses and crocodiles. Nobles would spend an afternoon hunting in these reed beds, moving silently in flatbottomed boats among the scented lotus flowers. They threw sticks to stun or kill birds. Sometimes they speared fish or used a **harpoon** to kill a hippopotamus.

Hunters feared the crocodile, which has now disappeared from Egypt. It would sometimes attack a cow drinking water at the edge of the river or even a boat. Many people believed that the crocodile was the water god Sobk in a changed form.

▽ Hunters traveling through the reed beds in a boat made of papyrus. In the water beneath the boat you can see a crocodile and the hippopotamus they are hunting.

Meat for the table

△ A herdsman shows geese in a basket to an official who will count them and judge their quality.

▽ The man on the left is forcing the crane to eat the bread to make it fatter.

Many birds were caught live and then fattened up. They were forced to eat small lumps of bread that had been soaked in oil and wine. Ducks, geese, and even pelicans were also kept for their eggs. In scenes of banquets in Ancient Egypt there is sometimes a large roast goose on the table. At other feasts, pigeons or quails were eaten.

Most of the land in Egypt had to be used to grow crops to feed people. There was not much space left for grazing animals. Only rich people ate meat regularly. Ordinary people did not eat much meat from cattle, sheep, and goats, but many workers kept pigs. Some of the priests of the time told people not to eat pork or fish, but it is certain that many people did so.

Pork and fish do not keep well in hot climates. In Ancient Egypt there was no good way of keeping food cold and fresh for long. Once pork and fish went bad, the smell was terrible.

Herbs and flavorings

Egyptians made oil from seeds such as sesame or from balsam and linseed. They also cooked sheep's tails, and melted, or

Ancient Egyptians were fond of the sweet smells, or **fragrances**, of flowers and spices. These may have been necessary to hide the bad smell of rotting food!

In Ancient Egypt a guest would probably have been offered a piece of bread sprinkled with salt. A common snack today is *duklah*, a small packet of salt, pepper, and mint.

Medicines in Ancient Egypt used many herbs and other ingredients we know today: mustard seeds were said to cure aches and pains; poppy seeds were made into opium. Even castor oil and syrup from figs were known and used, but possibly for cooking as well as medicines.

◁ In this scene the goatherd (on the right) is carrying a bowl that probably contains milk or cheese.

rendered, them down into fat. This cooking fat was called *alya*.

Milk did not stay fresh for long in Egypt's heat. Goats' and sheep's milk was often made into yogurt to make it last longer. From this was made a creamy kind of cheese called *labna*, and a harder, thicker one called *gebna*.

Salt was widely used in Egypt. It added flavor and was used to preserve food, such as fish. Other herbs and seeds, including cumin, coriander, and sesame, were used in cooking.

Pepper and dried, ground peppercorns did not come to Egypt until much later. There is evidence that some of the spices used in today's Arab cooking were grown in Ancient Egypt—herbs such as dill, fennel, and the curry-smelling fenugreek. Strong flavors may have been needed to hide the fact that food started to go bad so quickly.

▷ The ducks have been split open and salted. They are being put into jars and will be kept. The salt preserves the meat and stops it from rotting.

Drinking

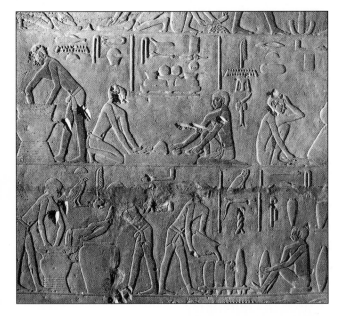

Most people drank beer in Ancient Egypt. Partly baked loaves of bread were broken up and water was added. The yeast in the bread and the warm climate made the mixture **ferment**. After a while, the thick mixture was strained through a sieve and left in a large pan. Later it would be put into small jars.

Fruits such as dates were added to the liquid for flavor. This made the beer dark and sweet. The bitter taste of modern beer is made by adding hops, which were not grown in Ancient Egypt at the time of the Nineteenth dynasty.

People drank beer at festivals, like the one held each year to praise the goddess Hathor.

△ The top picture shows workers making bread and then soaking it in water. The workers in the bottom picture are pouring the liquid into the jars where it will be kept.

▷ The workers on the left are stepping on grapes. The worker on the right will store the wine in jars.

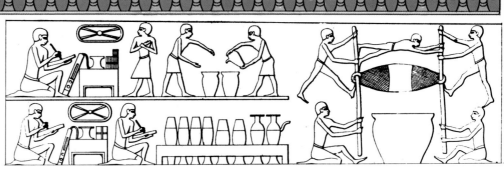

▷ The bag on the right of this picture contains the wine pulp. The workers are using sticks to twist the bag and squeeze out the last drops of grape juice.

Grapes for wine and feasts

How do we know that Egyptians grew vines and used grapes to make wines? Wild vine seeds were discovered in El Omari in pre-dynastic times. Many tombs contain the baskets and jars in which bunches of grapes and dried grapes, or raisins, were carried and served at the table. In the famous tomb of King Tutankhamen, an **alabaster** jar was found with sugary remains in it. This was probably grape juice or wine. Many carvings and paintings show the harvesting and pressing of grapes.

Looking after the vines in the hot climate was hard work. The vines had to be watered very often. This meant that only the rich people could afford to grow them. Sometimes the grapes were grown on bushes and hedges, but often the vines were made to grow up and across long branches. These branches were called **trellises**.

At harvest time the grapes were picked and put into a large container called a **vat**. The workers crushed the grapes by stepping on them with their bare feet. The juice from the grapes ran down a pipe and was collected. The warm climate probably made the juice start to ferment. Once the wine was ready it was put into pottery jars. No one yet knew how to make glass, and quite soon the wine would begin to seep through the sides of the jar. Most wine could not be kept for long, and had to be drunk "young." Some wines were made from plums and pomegranates.

△ A pottery drinking cup, made around 1900 B.C.

Wines were sometimes mixed together for a feast. At a feast, wine was drunk in large quantities. Musicians would make guests sad with songs about death and the need to live life to the fullest. No one refused a bowl of wine, and by the end of the evening it was sometimes true that, as one writer said, "the banquet is disordered by drunkenness."

▽ A fine wine chalice, or cup, made around 1200 B.C. of faience pottery.

Houses and homes

Ancient Egyptians lived in many different types of homes, depending on how rich they were. Very poor workers, called fellahins, might live in huts made from the mud of the Nile. In this small, one-room house, the family cooked, ate, and slept. Rich nobles lived in large houses or palaces with many rooms.

△ This model shows a village house, with offerings of food for the dead in the courtyard.

The houses of ordinary workers have not survived, so we can only guess how they looked. They may have been made from mud, wood, and reeds. Some pottery models of small houses have been found in tombs. They are called "soul houses," and they show how a fairly wealthy farming family lived.

Carvings and pictures in the tombs of rich people tell us how they lived and what their houses looked like. Some tombs were even

▽ People sitting in front of a table, with food offerings for the gods.

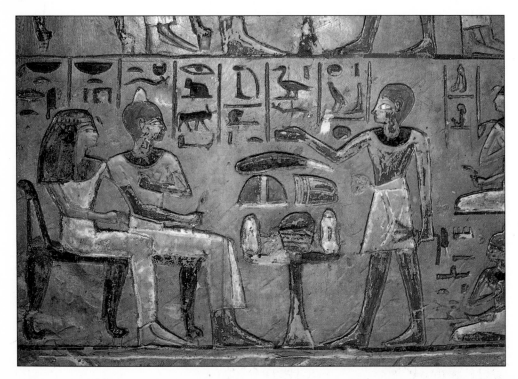

made to look like houses. Archaeologists have been able to reconstruct the layout of rich people's homes from this information. Kitchens were built away from the house or sometimes on the roof (there was no danger of rain!). This meant that the house did not smell of cooking or fill with smoke. There was also less risk of fire.

△ A model of the official's estate at Tell al-'Amarna.

Layout of a large house

Archaeologists have been able to put together plans that show the way a big house was arranged. The guests moved from room to room during a special feast.

At the site of the city of Tell al-'Amarna, we can tell how a noble family in the Twelfth dynasty lived and ate. The servants looked after the food and drink for this household. The chief of the household was called the "superintendent of the provision house." He was in charge of the storerooms, the bakery, and the slaughterhouse, where the animals were killed and prepared for cooking.

At the head of the kitchen was the "superintendent of the dwelling." The slaves worked under him. The "superintendent of the bakehouse" was in charge of the bakery, and there was even a "scribe of the sideboard" who took charge of his master's drinks. These were often served to guests by young girls and boys, known as the "bearers of cool drinks."

▷ In this carving you can see a servant looking after the fire in the kitchen. Wine is kept in storage jars called **amphorae**.

Cooking, food, and feasts

▷ The round loaves are cooked on the outside of the stove. Bread of all shapes and sizes is stored on the bakery shelves. At the bottom are jars of beer.

▽ A pottery storage jar that was made around 1400 B.C.

In the time of the Old Empire, Egyptians sat on the floor or squatted to eat their meals. People helped themselves from a low table in the middle of the floor. They ate with their hands. Later paintings show guests at feasts sitting on high, cushioned chairs and being served by slaves.

The bakery and the storehouse were often next to the kitchen. Food was cooked on an open fire or on a stove shaped like a cone or cylinder. Cooking pots were made of clay, and many kitchen tools were made of wood. There were some knives, made of the metals copper and bronze. Many people still used sharp stone, called **flint**, to make tools to cut food.

In great houses or at special meals, the dining hall would be decorated with wreaths

◁ A painted carving showing food being prepared and fish being cooked.

◁ These drawings from wall paintings show people at a feast. On the top row you can see figs, the wing of a goose, and a joint of meat. On the bottom row you can see a fish, someone drinking water, and more figs.

There is a wall picture in Thebes that gives some idea of what a feast was like in the house of a rich family. In the open porch in front of the house are the wine jars. The food is already on the table, which is decorated with flower garlands. Many jars, loaves, and bowls are close by. The guests greet their host as they arrive, and two servants wait in the background. The servants are helping themselves to some of the food!

and garlands of flowers. Long, low benches, or **couches**, were laid out, and jars of wines opened. Bowls of fruit were placed on a big table in the middle of the room, while roast meats and other foods were put on low tables.

Some houses had very large numbers of servants. Toward the end of a meal, a servant would bring a jug of scented water and a bowl for the guests to wash their hands.

▽ A basket from Saqqara, from around 600 B.C.

Feasts

We think of a feast as a celebration, and many of those held in Ancient Egypt were. Some took place at harvest time, or to thank the gods and goddesses for a good flooding of the Nile River.

Feasts in Egyptian palaces were very grand. At harvest time, people first made offerings to thank the god Min for good crops. Then they celebrated, thanking the goddesses of pleasure, Hathor and Bastet. They danced and shouted

▷ Dancers and musicians performing at a feast. Drinks are being served to the women guests.

△ The women at this feast are handing flowers to each other to smell. They are being anointed with sweet oils.

Before the feast, people bathed their bodies in ointments. Flowers were important at a feast. People wore sweet-smelling blossoms in their hair and sometimes necklaces or garlands of lotus flowers. Both women and men wore makeup and wigs for special events.

for joy. Music and singing were an important part of a feast. People ate, drank, and talked, while music was played in the background. Young boys and girls danced to entertain the diners.

In rich houses and palaces, people took a long time to prepare for a feast. Men and women wore special clothes for the occasion. These were made of linen and were long and loose, to keep the wearer cool in the heat. Sometimes the clothes were pleated and draped, and women's robes might be embroidered with beads. Everyone wore lots of jewelry, which might be made of gold or silver or simple shells and polished stones.

A favorite dish at an Egyptian feast was *ferique*. This was a stew made with chicken, calves' feet, and eggs in their shells. It was thickened with grain.

▷ Reaching for figs at a table.

A huge amount of food was served at feasts. A whole ox might be cooked, since beef was a luxury meat. People enjoyed roast goose, and pictures show ducks, quails, and pigeon stews. The food was not served with sauces or gravy. Vegetables and bread were offered to the guests. They ate with their fingers, but most people used plates, cups, and dishes. In rich houses these might be made of gold or silver instead of pottery.

△ A fruit and flower bowl, made around 1700 B.C.

During a feast, a cone of scented wax was placed on the guests' wigs. The wax slowly melted in the heat and gave out pleasant smells. One writer called it, "a fine drizzle of beauteous odors."

A famous banquet

A famous banquet took place at Saqqara in Ancient Egypt, and a clear and detailed wall painting of it can be seen in the British Museum in London. In it, you can see men and women eating, drinking, singing, and dancing.

Serving boys and girls went around offering bowls of wine. The dancers were beautifully dressed in girdles and a thin transparent cloak. They mingled with the diners and were a central part of the feast. Musicians played lutes, lyres, and flutes and sang songs about living life to the fullest.

By the end of the evening, it seems people had often had too much to drink. Some guests were in a state of collapse!

▷ The picture on the top shows musicians and dancers entertaining a group of guests. The guests seem to be smelling flowers while they watch and listen. In the lower picture, bowls of wine are being passed around by a young boy. In the corner are tables loaded with food for the feast.

Food for the next world

▷ This collection of food was an offering to the gods. It included loaves of bread, pieces of duck, and dried fish.

The food and drink that were placed in Egyptian tombs tell us a great deal about the food people ate when they were alive.

The Ancient Egyptians believed that dead people passed into another, everlasting life. They would need help from the gods and

▷ Wine is being offered before Osiris, the chief god of the kingdom of the dead.

▷ In this picture the people are going to the funeral by boat. You can see the wrapped body, called a **mummy**, in the coffin. Underneath the coffin are bags containing offerings for the gods.

goddesses to make the journey from this life into the next one. They would also need food for the journey and all kinds of things for their next life. Their families provided food for them, and they also offered food to the gods, asking them to protect the person who had died.

The menu of a funeral meal, which was prepared for a king in the Nineteenth dynasty, has survived. By this time, many foods and wines were brought into Egypt by merchants from other countries. The menu includes: well-baked loaves from fine corn, good wine and beer, fine oil and the best figs. These offerings came from other countries, including Jordan and what is now Iran.

▽ This wooden model shows a man carrying an amphora of food or drink as a funeral offering.

Food for a funeral

At a funeral it was often the custom to slaughter a large ox or gazelle. The beast would be tied up and its main vein, the **jugular**, cut. The animal would be slit open and the heart removed. This was considered the most delicious part of the animal. The legs would then be cut off, and these and other parts of the body would be put in the tomb as an offering.

Many of the remaining pieces of the animal were then cooked and used to feed the people who had come to the funeral procession. Nothing was ever wasted. The Ancient Egyptians were above all a practical people.

Meals and recipes

Some of the dishes eaten in Ancient Egypt, such as hummus, are popular today. As far as we know, the Ancient Egyptians did not write down recipes or use cookbooks, but many of the ingredients used by them are still important in Egyptian cooking. The ingredients in today's recipes are similar but the taste may be different from dishes served in Ancient Egypt.

The ways we preserve foods today, by canning and freezing, had not been invented in those days. The taste of foods that have been preserved by drying, salting, or pickling is quite different from those that are canned or frozen.

The Ancient Egyptians ground their cooking ingredients by hand. Because of this, the texture of their bread was rough and gritty. They were unlikely to have made smooth, fine mixtures of ingredients for their dishes, as we do now, using machines such as food processors.

The choice of fresh fruit, vegetables, and herbs depended on what was grown after the yearly floods. Radishes, cucumbers, onions, and garlic seem to have been important foods for working people. Melons, dates, figs, and pomegranates were grown in Ancient Egypt and were popular fruits at feasts.

Olives were not grown in Ancient Egypt, so there was no olive oil. Instead, people made oil from sesame seeds. Citrus fruits, such as lemons, were not grown, so there was no lemon juice. Sour wine or wine vinegar may have been used instead. Honey was used to sweeten dishes.

> **WARNING:** Sharp knives and boiling liquids are dangerous. Hot ovens and pans can burn you. *Always ask an adult to help you* when you are preparing or cooking food in the kitchen.

Ingredients

1 cup canned
   garbanzo beans

juice of 1 lemon *or*
   2 T lemon juice

3 cloves of garlic

5 T tahini (sesame
   seed paste)

1 tsp salt

fresh parsley

Sharp knives are
dangerous.

Equipment

measuring cup

large mixing bowl

cup

strainer

sharp knife

cutting board

lemon squeezer

wooden spoon

mortar and pestle *or*
   food processor

serving dish

Hummus bi Tahini (Garbanzo beans and sesame dip)

The dish can be decorated with fresh sprigs of parsley. You can serve the dish with vegetables or pita bread.

1. Drain the liquid from the garbanzo beans into a cup. Put the garbanzo beans into a large mixing bowl.
2. Peel the cloves of garlic and chop them very finely. Take care to keep your fingers away from the blade of the knife. Add the garlic to the garbanzo beans.
3. If you are using fresh lemons rather than lemon juice, use a lemon squeezer to get the juice out of the lemons. Add the lemon juice to the garbanzo beans.
4. Add the tahini paste and salt to the garbanzo beans with a little of the garbanzo bean liquid. Stir the mixture thoroughly.
5. Spoon the mixture into the mortar and use the pestle to crush it into a thick paste *or* ask an adult to blend it in a food processor for you.
6. Add a little more garbanzo bean liquid if the mixture is too stiff.
7. Taste the mixture and add more salt if necessary.
8. Put the mixture into a serving dish and decorate the dish with fresh parsley. Serve it with vegetables or pita bread.

Ful Medames

Today this is Egypt's national dish and is usually served at breakfast time. The main hot dish is served with a choice of cold garnishes in small bowls, for people to help themselves. These include: whole hard boiled eggs, chopped onions sprinkled with salt, chopped pickled or fresh cucumber, chopped parsley, slices of fresh lemon. Seasonings such as salt, pepper, ground cumin seeds, and olive oil are also put on the table.

Ingredients

1 cup dried lima or
   fava beans

$1/2$ cup dried red
   lentils

4 cloves of garlic

salt to taste

vegetables and
   seasonings of
   your choice for
   the garnishes to
   the main dish

1. Put the dried beans and lentils into a mixing bowl and cover them with at least one inch of cold water. Let them soak overnight.
2. Drain the beans and lentils. Then rinse them.
3. Peel the cloves of garlic and then chop them coarsely. Take care to keep your fingers away from the blade of the knife.
4. Put the lentils, beans, and garlic into a saucepan and just cover them with water.
5. Bring the water to a boil and then lower the heat. Cook the beans and lentils slowly for about $4^{1}/2$ to 5 hours until tender. Stir from time to time.
6. When the beans are cooked remove the saucepan from the heat. Stir in salt to taste.
7. Prepare the garnishes to go with the main dish and put them in small bowls.
8. Pour the bean and lentil mixture into a serving dish or bowls and serve warm.

Equipment

large mixing bowl

colander

large saucepan

sharp knife

cutting board

small bowls

serving dish *or*
   bowls

**Ask an adult to
help you when you
start to cook.**

Hot liquids and
pans are dangerous.

Radish salad

Ingredients

10 radishes

1 T chopped fresh
   parsley

2 T olive oil *or*
   sesame seed oil

1 T lemon juice *or*
   wine vinegar

salt to taste

1. Wash the radishes in cold water. Make sure no dirt is left on them. Then carefully chop off the leaves and roots. Take care to keep your fingers away from the blade of the knife.
2. Chop the radishes coarsely and put them in the serving bowl.
3. Chop the fresh parsley finely and add it to the radishes.
4. Add the lemon juice *or* wine vinegar and olive oil *or* sesame seed oil to the salad and stir all the ingredients together.
5. Add salt to taste and serve at once.

Equipment

cutting board

sharp knife

wooden spoon

serving bowl

Sharp knives are
dangerous.

Cucumber and yogurt

Ingredients

$1^{1}/2$ cups plain
   yogurt

3 T chopped fresh
   mint

salt

2 cloves garlic

1 cucumber

This dish can be served as a dip with vegetables or pita bread or as a side dish to accompany your main meal.

1. Chop the fresh mint finely. Take care to keep your fingers away from the blade of the knife.
2. Pour the yogurt into the serving bowl. Add the chopped mint and a pinch of salt.
3. Beat the mixture with a whisk until it is smooth and thin. Taste it and add more salt if necessary.

Equipment

measuring cup

cutting board

sharp knife

whisk

potato peeler

wooden spoon

serving bowl

Sharp knives are
dangerous.

4. Use the potato peeler to peel the cucumber. Then carefully cut the cucumber into small cubes with a knife.
5. Peel the cloves of garlic and chop them coarsely.
6. Stir the garlic and cucumber into the yogurt mixture with a wooden spoon.
7. Chill the mixture in the refrigerator for about an hour.

Honey date cake

Ingredients

3/4 cup wholewheat flour

1 T cooking oil

1/2 cup clear honey

1/4 cup pitted dates

1 egg

1 tsp mixed spices

Ask an adult to help you when you start to cook.

Hot liquids, pans, and ovens are dangerous.

1. Preheat oven to 400°F.
2. Sift the flour into a mixing bowl.
3. Whisk the egg in another bowl.
4. Put the the honey and oil into a small saucepan on a very low heat. Do not let the honey boil or burn. Stir the mixture until the honey melts. Then take the saucepan off the heat.
5. Add the honey mixture and the beaten egg to the flour. Beat the mixture into a dough with the whisk.
6. Mash the dates using a mortar and pestle or ask an adult to mash them for you in a food processor.
7. Add the mashed dates and mixed spices to the dough. Blend them in well using a wooden spoon.
8. Shape the mixture into 8 flat cakes.
9. Place on a baking sheet and put in oven for about 25-30 minutes. Ask an adult to do this for you.

Equipment

measuring cup

strainer

large mixing bowl

whisk

small mixing bowl

small saucepan

wooden spoon

mortar and pestle *or* food processor

baking sheet

cooling rack

plate or serving dish

Dried fruit salad

Ingredients

1 cup dried apricots

1/2 cup dried prunes

1/2 cup dried figs

1/4 cup raisins

1/3 cup clear honey

1 T rose water

water

Today chopped nuts, such as almonds, pine nuts, or pistachios, are added to this salad. You can add your favorite dried fruits to it as well. The ingredients given here are ones that the Ancient Egyptians may have used.

1. Put the dried fruits into a sieve. Wash them in cold water and drain them.
2. Put the fruits in a large serving bowl. Stir in the honey and rose water.
3. Add cold water, until the fruit is covered. Leave the fruit to soak for at least 48 hours.
4. Stir the mixture and then serve.

Equipment

measuring cup

sieve

large serving bowl

wooden spoon

Glossary

alabaster: Soft white stone that can be easily carved and polished.

amphorae: Tall, narrow jars made of pottery, used to store liquids such as wine.

archaeologists: People who study the past by digging up or examining ancient ruins and remains.

baited: Food that is put on or into a trap, to catch fish or animals.

banquet: A grand feast or public dinner.

bartering: A form of buying and selling by exchanging goods.

couch: A long, comfortable seat for two or more people.

dough: A mixture of flour, water, and sometimes salt. Bread is made by adding yeast to the mixture and baking it in the oven.

dynasty: A series of rulers who are members of the same family, or the period of time during which members of the same family rule.

excavate: To dig up buried objects in a scientific manner, in order to find out more about the past.

ferment: Food is chemically changed when gases get into it. This can be caused by adding yeast, or the change can happen naturally, if food is left uncovered.

fertile: Rich in the nutrients that help plants to grow.

flint: A type of stone that splits easily into sharp-edged pieces.

fragrances: Pleasant smells, such as those of flowers or spices.

funerary offerings: Objects placed in the grave of dead persons when they are buried.

game: Animals, birds, or fish that are hunted for food and for sport.

harpoon: A type of spear attached to a long rope, used for catching fish and other sea animals.

hieroglyphs: The small picture symbols used in Ancient Egyptian writing. The symbols represent words and sounds.

inundation: The flooding of land along the Nile River, which happened every year in September and October in Ancient Egypt.

irrigate: To bring water to crops.

jugular: One of the large veins on each side of the neck.

monuments: Buildings or statues that have been put up to remind people of a special event or person.

mummy: A dead body that has been preserved with ointments and wrapped tightly in thin strips of cloth.

papyrus: A type of reed that grows in and around the Nile River. Papyrus was used to make paper. The reeds were peeled and cut into strips. The strips were soaked in water to make them soft, then placed across one another, pressed, and dried to form a sheet.

pyramid: A massive stone building with a square base and four triangular sides.

render: To melt (fat) down to a liquid.

scribe: Someone whose job is to write things out by hand or to keep written records.

sickle: A tool with a curved blade and a short handle, used for cutting back undergrowth and harvesting crops.

trellises: Pieces of wood that are fastened together to support plants.

vat: A large tub made of wood or stone in which wine or other drinks are made or stored.

Further reading

Caselli, Giovanni. *The Everyday Life of the Egyptian Craftsman.* New York: Peter Bedrick Books, 1991.

Fleming, Stuart. *The Egyptians.* New York: New Discovery Books, 1992.

Ganeri, Anita. *Focus on Ancient Egyptians.* New York: Gloucester Press, 1993.

Hart, George. *Ancient Egypt.* San Diego: Harcourt Brace Jovanovich, 1989.

Koening, Viviane. *The Ancient Egyptians: Life in the Nile Valley.* Brookfield, Conn.: Millbrook Press, 1992.

Oliphant, Margaret. *The Egyptian World.* New York: Franklin Watts, 1989.

Sauvain, Philip. *Over 3,000 Years Ago: In Ancient Egypt.* New York: New Discovery Books, 1993.

Steele, Philip. *The Egyptians and the Valley of the Kings.* New York: Dillon Press, 1994.

Index